Training Super Service Dogs

How to Train The Most Supportive Service Dog And Companion Volume 1

Chris Peyton

contents

Introduction

With the ongoing pandemic, the elderly and disabled need more than ever of adequate resources for living assistance.

Whether it is due to being a demographic more susceptible to infection, or increased isolation due to lockdown, the more vulnerable among us need resources and tools to deal with the daily challenges they encounter.

As with everything, nature provides a solution. And one of the best solutions comes in the form of everyone's favorite 4-legged creature that has come to be known as "man's best friend". If you read the title of this book, then you know exactly what creature I'm talking about.... I'm talking about dogs! And not just any dogs, but dogs that can become super service dogs!

If you've ever seen someone train a dog to do tricks, you'll know that dogs can be trained to do some wild stuff! We can take that same ability to train dogs and implement it with assisted living. For the elderly and the disabled, you can truly see why dogs make such great companions.

For many people, having a service dog is the difference between living and dying. Not only do service dogs help to prevent physical injury, but also emotional issues as well. With the quarantine situation worldwide, there is a rise in depression and suicide. As you can imagine, the most vulnerable in our society suffer more than the general population and often don't have the assistance they need and deserve.

In either case, dogs are wonderful companions. And what this book aims to do is help those who are affected by disabilities to train a lifelong friend that you can depend on for life. A super service dog that can not only help you with your daily tasks but will rescue you if needed, just like a true superhero would, in case you ever find yourself truly in need of it.

Keep in mind this is only volume 1. This volume is dedicated to mastering the fundamentals. If you feel your skills with dog training are beyond this manual, then I would recommend purchasing volume 2 (or get both volumes in one), in which we discuss the more advanced commands and tasks and prepare you to take the public access test.

Please keep in mind that taking the public access test is not legally required. Still, the certification can be beneficial in the situation that anyone tries to give you trouble about your service dog when you are in public. For this reason, we recommend taking the public access test, but please do remember that it is not legally required for you to be in public with your service dog; it's just a helpful bonus.

When you are preparing to train your dog to become a service dog, there are two double d's you must consider the disability and the dog. You must think about what type of disability the person the dog will be assisting might have, regardless of whether it is you or a loved one. You want to have a clear idea of the types of tasks your new service dog will be expected to perform.

So, of course, you then have to consider the dog. You want to make sure you get a breed of dog that is physically capable of doing everything expected of him during his service dog duties.

For example, if you need help lifting and moving heavy objects, a chihuahua is probably not the best choice for you as far as a service dog goes! In this book, we individualize some exercises into four main categories:

1. ambulatory (meaning able to walk without aid)
2. Ambulatory with devices (which includes crutches, canes, walkers, etc.)
3. Manual wheelchair
4. Power chair (this includes all types of electric wheelchairs and scooters)

After you've decided what kind of dog to train based upon the type of disability you are dealing with, the next thing to remember before you begin is this motto. "attitude is everything!"

In college, I had a math professor that used math to show that attitude makes a 100% difference. He showed that if you took each letter in the word "attitude" and added each letter's numerical equivalent, meaning a=1, b=2, c=3,..., z=26, "attitude" added up to 100 while other words like "knowledge" only added to 96 and "hard work" only added to 98.

While this is a cute little example, it represents universal truth. Our attitude about something can be the difference between one of the best days of our lives and one of the worst. The power and influence of our attitude are especially true when we are working with animals. Dogs have strong intuition and are very in tune with human emotions. Whatever attitude you have is going to be reflected in your dog's behavior.

So if you have a positive attitude when training your dog, your dog will learn to love working with you and assisting you. And conversely, if you have a negative attitude and try to use fear to force your dog into submission, you aren't going to have trained a loyal lifelong companion. You're going to have trained a scared servant who may not listen to you consistently. So remember, attitude is everything!

Another motto to remember when training your service dog is "haste makes waste, so slow is fast." We have all struggled with being patient with something, and in this day and age, with attention spans shorter than ever, patience is at an all-time low. But when you are training your service dog, you are going to have to learn patience.

You will find a little patience will go a long way when working on having your dog master certain tasks. Consistency and patience are your two keys to success with dog training in general and especially with service dog training.

Before we get started with discussing the different training methods, we will just take a quick side note to let you know that when we refer to a general service dog with the pronoun "he," we are doing so for simplicity's sake. Both male and female dogs can make wonderful service dogs, and gender isn't a relevant factor.

The last thing you need to remember when training your dog is to enjoy yourself. Have fun. Remember that the better your attitude, the better the training will go. With that last friendly reminder, we are ready to jump into the first thing to learn when training your dog, and that is how to give praise.

Chapter 1: how to praise your dog

"praise is the most important part of dog training." -Lydia kelly

I will let you know right now that if giving praise is something you are shy about doing or have a hard time doing, then you need to get yourself comfortable with giving praise before you can even think about training your service dog.

Giving your dog praise is so important because it is the praise that motivates your dog. Think of praise as similar to your dog's paycheck. Let me ask you a question: if you didn't have a consistent paycheck at a job you worked, would you put forth consistent effort? The honest answer is probably not.

So with this in mind, if you don't give consistent praise, your dog's behavior won't be consistent either. What you want is for your dog to associate receiving praise and org successfully carrying out a command. In psychology, this concept is known as positive reinforcement, and positive reinforcement is one of the most important tools in your dog training toolkit.

Now, one thing people will often worry about is giving their dog too much praise. While this can happen, what happens more often is that dog owners don't give enough praise or even that the praise given isn't enthusiastic enough.

The main thing you want to pay attention to is giving too much praise when the praise isn't appropriate. You want the praise to be associated with the dog successfully following your command. If you give praise in any given situation, the praise loses its meaning.

So if you have a particular voice you use or signal you give when you praise your dog, make sure only to use that voice or signal when your dog follows your commands successfully or makes appropriate progress in learning commands. Don't worry. When we go over each command in this book, we will talk about when to praise during training.

It's important to remember that no matter how well your dog has learned a command, always always praise your dog after they have done something you wanted. As we said in the introduction, consistency is one of the keys to successful dog training.

I can't stress enough that if you aren't comfortable giving praise, you want to get comfortable with giving praise before you start training a service dog. If you have to lock yourself in your room for hours on end practicing giving praise, then do so.

When giving praise, remember it's not the words you say that matter but the tone of your voice. A high-pitched, excited, and bubbly tone communicates that you are happy with your dog's actions, so this is typically the best kind of tone to use when giving praise.

If you deal with any speech impediments or difficulties, remember that the tone you use is the most important part. So if you can give an audible signal in an appropriate tone, you don't have to worry. If you have difficulty making any audible noise, tools such as clickers and bells are great alternatives to give your dog praise. This brings us to the next big tool for giving praise. Food.

Chapter 2: using food as a reward and praise

"don't bite the hand that feeds you." -ancient proverb

There is probably nothing more powerful than food when it comes to tools for positive reinforcement in dog training. However, with great power comes great responsibility. So when using food as a training tool, you don't want to use it if your dog can't control himself whenever you pull food out.

I would highly recommend getting your dog used to you bringing out food from your pocket before using food as a regular training tool. Specifically, your dog should not be jumping all over you just because you have food in your hand. When your dog has learned not to do this, I recommend using food as a regular training tool, especially for the more complex tasks.

So if you have a dog that jumps on you anytime you reach to pull out food, you'll want to address that before trying to use food as a regular tool for positive reinforcement training. Essentially, you don't want to make a big deal out of having food. Again attitude is everything. If you have a calm and relaxed attitude about having food, your dog will see that and will come to reflect that calm attitude as well.

If your dog keeps jumping up on you every time he sees you with food, then you want to condition the dog to be calm in the presence of food. You can do this by first bringing out food from your pocket and if your dog jumps on you, correct that behavior first by firmly telling your dog "no!" Or "off!"

Then you will want to put the food back in your pocket and ignore your dog's begging until he realizes that he isn’t going to get the food and calms down. Depending on just how excited your dog gets around food, it may take several days to condition your dog's behavior around food properly, but, as always, consistency is key!

Once your dog has learned to be calm around food, you can start using food as a reward to accompany praise during training. Many trainers will tell you timing is everything, insinuating that if you are too slow with your response to your dog, he won’t properly associate the food reward with the action. This idea, however, is a misconception. It is more about pace and the sequence of events than the amount of time between events when it comes to timing.

This is important to remember for training service dogs in particular because people can have disabilities that require them to operate at a slower pace, and people should know that this is fine. The food reward needs to follow your dog successfully performing the desired task, and always remember that when you give food rewards, you give it after verbal praise.

Remember, the praise is your dog's paycheck. The food reward is more like a very generous bonus for a job well done.

If your dog tries to nip at you as he takes the treat, pull your hand back and say "easy" or something similar. Don't pull away fast.

Remember, attitude is everything. If you act like you have to take away the treat, your dog is much more likely to jump at you for it. So just close your fingers around the treat, calmly pull back and say, "easy." Don't give your dog the food reward if he is nipping.

When he stops nipping, say “good easy,” and open your fingers to give him the treat.

If you cannot hold food for whatever reason, there are dispenser devices that you can use, and you may be able to devise some method of giving food as a reward. Try different methods to see what works best for your particular situation. If you have to enlist the help of someone else as a last resort, you need to make sure the praise comes from you. And you need to make sure to teach whoever is helping you to give food at the appropriate time. Again this should be after you have given the verbal praise.

Another great thing about food is that it can be used to facilitate bonding. If you are the one who feeds your dog his meals, then your bond is certain to be stronger than if someone else feeds your dog. If it’s the case that someone else feeds your dog, then I would highly recommend that you are at least present with your dog during his meals.

Make sure all communications come from you and that you remain close while your dog is eating. Be aware that you don't overfeed your dog. On days you choose to use food as a reward during training, make sure to give him a little less supper to compensate.

On the off chance your dog isn't that into food rewards, you should find some other reward that your dog is more excited about. Remember, every dog is different and will exhibit slightly different behaviors, which brings us to chapter 3.

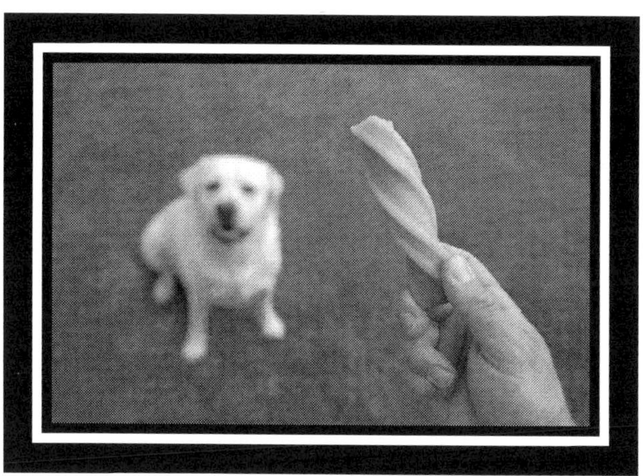

Chapter 3: analyzing the behavior

"one thing I believe strongly in this life is that you just don't reward bad behavior."

-dr. Phil

At some point, we've all played the role of a psychologist and have tried to psychoanalyze the behavior of our friends and family.

Well, if that's something you're into, then I've got good news for you: you get to do the same thing with your dog! The only difference is your dog is, well, a dog and not a human.

Dogs and humans have a very special relationship that spans most of our evolutionary history, and some dog owners will swear their dog knows what they are thinking. However, it would help if you always remembered that dogs aren't humans, and they don't think in human terms, and we humans have a bad habit of seeing everything from a human lens.

Since your dog is not a human, you can't analyze the dog's behavior in the same way. This means you have to take the time to observe and learn your dog's behavior. What things does your dog seem to like? What things is your dog scared of?

Once you get a sense of what behaviors your dog is prone to, you need to figure out which behaviors are appropriate and inappropriate. You have to begin training your dog to know which behaviors are allowed and which behaviors aren't. Generally speaking, basic obedience training is usually enough to manage the most common dog behaviors that could be a problem. Now let's talk a bit about just how dogs think.

As you probably are aware, dogs are descended from wolves. If you didn't know that, well, now you know why dogs and wolves look so similar as if they are related. Since dogs are descended from wolves, they are pack animals by nature, and as pack animals, dogs naturally look for a leader of their pack.

When you observe any pack animals in a group, the leader is usually very easy to pick out. The pack leader will appear more dominant, and the other pack members will display submissive behavior simply at a glance from the pack leader. So since dogs think in a pack mentality, who does your dog view as the pack leader?

The correct answer should be you! To ensure obedience and submission, you must be the leader of the pack. Again, this should not be done through the use of intimidation and punishment, but you must still display a level of dominance and authority with your dog. Typically, unless you have a very dominant dog, your dog will accept you as the pack leader if you are fair and consistent with your obedience training.

On the off chance that you do have a very dominant dog that growls at you during training, trying to challenge you for dominance, I recommend you seek a professional dog behaviorist for help. And I highly recommend you find a behaviorist that does not resort to physical punishment in training, as this can worsen the problem.

This is a good segue into the idea of knowing the characteristics of your dog's breed. This can give you invaluable insight into the behaviors and potential behaviors of your dog. It would be too much to try to include information on every dog breed out there, so I would recommend trying to learn basic information from online sources about your dog’s breed.

It’s often said that 90% of communication is nonverbal. Whether that exact percentage is accurate, it can’t be denied that humans communicate a lot through body language, and the same is true for dogs. Most of us have heard the idea that if a dog is wagging its tail, that means the dog is happy. However, many more subtle body movements communicate a lot about your dog’s mood and desires, so pay close attention.

How you react to these signals is critical for developing your relationship with your dog. If your dog exhibits submissive behavior, you must use a controlled tone when correcting your dog's behavior. If you yell or scream at a submissive dog that is urinating on the carpet, you'll just increase the dog's fear, making the dog urinate longer.

As you become familiar with your dog's behavioral cues, you will be able to interrupt an action before it begins. You don't even have to correct your dog; you can just transfer your dog's actions to more acceptable behavior, which leads us to a very common method of dealing with certain behaviors called transference.

Transference is a training method where you take an unacceptable behavior your dog does and get your dog to replace that behavior with an acceptable alternative. For example, if your dog tries to jump up on visitors, you can train the dog to play with a toy when visitors come over as an acceptable alternative.

Now we will talk about a few examples of common behaviors most dog owners will wish to address. The first situation we will discuss is dealing with separation anxiety.

Since dogs are pack animals, they aren't built to spend long amounts of time alone. So when you leave your dog at home, it's natural for your dog to become anxious, especially initially since your dog doesn't know when or if you will return. The most common behaviors dogs do to express this anxiety are barking and chewing, so try to keep shoes out of your dog's reach when training them to stay home alone.

If you come home and you see your dog has chewed on something or had an accident, don't give in to the instinct to yell. Your dog won't know what he did wrong and will simply think it's dangerous to be around you when you return from being gone.

When you leave, you should have a phrase that your dog will come to associate with you leaving but returning later. "I'll be back", "guard the house", etc. Any phrase will work, really; you only have to use it consistently.

You want to gradually increase the amount of time you leave your dog by themselves. You will want to start with just a few minutes. Just leave the house, walk around the block and come back.

Remember to use your phrase for leaving. Don't lock the door for the first few times because you want to try to sneak in. However, if you are in a wheelchair, especially an electric one, sneaking in will probably not be an option. Just proceed with leaving for a short period and then returning.

If you see your dog chewing something when you return, you can scold him with a “bad” or “what did you do?” As soon as your dog drops what he is chewing, you stop correcting. Quietly give praise if he comes to you. Gradually increase and vary the amount of time you are absent. Start with 5 minutes, then increase to 10 minutes, 30 minutes, etc., do this for several days, so your dog gets used to you being gone.

One thing you can do to deal with chew behavior due to separation anxiety is getting a chew toy, so if your dog is chewing on something he shouldn’t, you can scold him, then give him the chew toy and praise him when he takes it and chews instead. It's not a bad idea to have multiple chew toys. That way, you can rotate toys in case your dog starts to get bored of one. Next, we'll talk about how to train your dog not to jump up on other people.

Jumping up on people is one of the most challenging things to train your dog not to do, but if you wish to train a service dog, it's something you have to do because it is unacceptable behavior in public. It is very common for young dogs to want to do this because they have so much energy. Again patience and consistency will be key to successfully teaching your dog not to jump up on people.

Your instinct is to back up if a dog jumps on you, but this will only reinforce a dominant position for your dog. A scenario like this is where a wheelchair can be an advantage because you can use the chair to move forward towards your dog as he jumps. Doing so will surprise your dog and return you to the dominant position.

If your dog jumps on you from behind, then go back into him. The intent isn't to run over your dog but to show him that you are the pack leader. If you are fully ambulatory, taking a big step toward your dog will be as effective as the wheelchair.

Make sure that you have an "off" command, and make sure you say it in a deep, firm, and gruff voice and tone.

When giving the command, the second your dog's feet hit the ground, praise, "good off!" If your dog jumps back on you, repeat the command, move forward, and praise again when his feet hit the ground. If you aren't physically able to do this part of the training on your own, you should have a friend assist you while having your dog on a leash to assist with carrying out the training.

When teaching your dog not to jump up and down, you must be consistent! Specifically, you can't teach your dog it's inappropriate to jump on people but sometimes, let your dog do it and be rewarded. It has to be a strict rule with no exceptions. You can, however, teach your dog to jump on you at your command and only at your command.

Understanding this also means when visitors come over, they need to know not to let your dog jump on them, and they have to cooperate. It doesn't matter if "they don't mind." It's not about what they mind. It is about the type of relationship and behavior you and your dog are trying to build. You are trying to train a super service dog. And super service dogs are only the most well-mannered and well-behaved of dogs.

At the beginning of your training, you should have your dog on a leash when guests come over and command "off" as guests enter. Keep your dog far enough from your guests to prevent your dog from reaching the guests. If your dog tries to run towards the guests, your dog will reach the end of the leash, and he will be automatically corrected. Make sure to have some 'slack' on the leash, so you aren't in a tug of war with your dog, and consistently praise when your dog's feet touch the floor.

This is another instance when the transference technique can be very useful. You can transfer your dog's attention to another stimulus like a chew toy or ball. This is particularly useful for those who may find it difficult to hold onto a leash when training your dog to not jump on guests. Also, if you have taught your dog the sit command, this is a perfect command to give when guests are about to enter your home. Your dog can't jump if he is sitting.

The last behavior/condition we will discuss before discussing the different equipment used for service dog training is phobias. Typically, if your dog is afraid of something, it's not a big deal, but if your dog is afraid of an umbrella opening, it won't be easy to get your dog to cooperate with you if you need to be with your dog outside in the rain.

So the goal is to train your dog to overcome any phobias that might make it more difficult for him to work with you in certain instances. As usual, a gradual and consistent approach is best. You will want to build up your dog's exposure around whatever thing your dog is afraid of. If it's the opening of an umbrella, walk your dog around it to get a sense of his response.

If your dog backs away, do not say, "it's okay" you may have the desire to comfort your dog, but this will give positive reinforcement that tells your dog it's good to back away from the umbrella. Now it is helpful to talk to the umbrella in a happy and high-pitched voice, as silly as it might sound. Doing so associates a positive stimulus, your happy voice, with the umbrella, making your dog more comfortable around the umbrella.

Be patient and let your dog approach it on his own time. If he goes near it to sniff and inspect, praise immediately. Remember to praise your dog anytime he moves closer to the feared object.

Patience is key so take as much time as you need to get your dog used to the feared object. Remember that you can't rush overcoming fear.

You can apply this same method to any object in your house, like a vacuum cleaner; if your dog fears cars, training them to overcome that fear will be a little different. Now, most dogs love cars and don't have any problem riding, but on the off chance that your dog is afraid of cars, you again want to build up your dog's exposure to the car gradually.

Start by simply walking around your car with your dog like you did with the umbrella example. Then the next day, go out before your dog and open one of the car doors. Then walk around the car again with your dog. Move closer and closer to the car each day unless your dog becomes anxious. Again speaking in a happy tone around the car will help make your dog more comfortable. Next, we will go over some of the equipment there is for training your service dog.

Chapter 4: getting the right equipment

"it is essential to have good tools, but it is also essential that the tools should be used in the right way." -Wallace d. Wattles

As with any endeavor, you want to have the proper tools to get the best results. Most of us have a basic idea of what tools we need for dog training in general, collars, leashes, etc.

Below is a list of the types of equipment we will go over in this chapter.

- Collars
- Training collars
- Leashes
- Long lines
- Flexi-leashes
- Head halters

Collars

Your dog should be wearing some kind of buckle collar at all times. The collar should hold his county license and other identification in case your dog somehow gets lost. However, training collars should only be used for training and should never be left on your dog unattended.

Your dog's buckle collar should be snug enough that it won't slide off, but it shouldn't be tight around your dog's neck. Collars come in various materials. There are flat leather, rolled leather, or nylon collars. Pick whichever material works best for you and your dog.

Training Collars

Training collars have been a mainstay for obedience training for some time now. They are also known as choke collars, but don't let that name give you the wrong impression. These collars are not meant to choke your dog. Training collars should only feel tight on your dog if correctly put on, and if the collar is used correctly, it should never choke your dog.

A training collar is a tool meant for communication. The collar is meant to allow you to throw your dog off balance just for a second so you can get your dog's attention to instruct him on what he needs to do. The correct way to use the training collar is with the "jerk and release" method. This method is primarily used to teach the "heel" command. If your dog pulls ahead of you, you use the leash to pull the collar tight for a brief second and then immediately release it.

Making a good correction means that you will hear a noise from the collar, and so will your dog. If you hold on for more than a second, you not only lose the advantage of surprise, but you risk damaging your dog's larynx. A proper correction must always be followed by immediate praise. Now let's talk about putting on the training collar.

Training collars have two equal-sized metal rings, one on each end. To make a loop, hold one ring in each hand between your thumb and forefinger. Lower one ring the length of the chain, then feed the chain through that ring until the two rings come together. You should have a loop that you can slip over your dog's head. Make sure you put the collar on correctly. Otherwise, the chain won't properly loosen even though you released it.

When you put on the training collar, make sure you remove the regular buckle collar to avoid any chance of the regular collar catching on the training collar. It's also important that you get a collar that is the proper size for your dog. Typically you want a well-fitting collar, and good instructors will say that you want 2 to 3 inches of play, meaning when the collar is tight, there shouldn't be more than two to three inches of extra chain.

There are cases where a person isn't physically able to put on a well-fitting collar on their dog due to the nature of a disability they deal with. In this case, it's not uncommon for someone to use a collar that is too big for their dog so they can put the collar on their dog. You have to figure out what will work best for you and your dog's particular situation, regardless of what instructors say.

Leashes

A collar is not really of any use without a leash. It's best to own a few different kinds of leashes for different situations. The typical dog owner may just have one leash for their dog, but since your dog is a super service dog, it makes sense to have different types of leashes because you'll need different levels of control based on the situation.

Typically leashes will be made of leather or webbing. However, I wouldn't recommend these because they can be hard on your hands. As you can imagine, leashes come in a variety of lengths. A 4 to a 6-foot leash is the standard for obedience training. If that is too long, then a traffic leash may be a better option, only two feet. This length is much better for walking in crowds. Again, this is why I recommend having a few leashes handy since different situations will call for different things.

When you consider the leash's width, you don't want something so wide that it's unwieldy for you, but you don't want a leash so thin that it will be hard on your hands. Test out several leashes to find out what works best for you.

Long Lines

During training, a long line is primarily used in recall so that you can be farther than six feet from your dog but still maintain control. If your dog doesn't come when you call, you can use the line to bring your dog to you. A long line leash is also suitable for practicing the 'stay' exercise from longer distances. The long line leash brings the best of both worlds. Your dog has a greater sense of freedom, and you still have a sense of control.

Flexi-Leashes

Flexi-leashes are retractable long line leashes. So you can operate it as a long line or a short line depending on the situation.

Flexi-leashes typically come with a plastic case with a handle and thumb button that loosens and retracts the leash line. A thin nylon line comes out of the case with a snap that attaches to your dog's collar. When your dog comes towards you, the line will retract automatically. The advantage of the Flexi-leash is, of course, its adjustable length. A Flexi-leash can give you the leash length you need in any situation.

Head Halters

Now that we've talked about collars and leashes let's discuss an alternative to the typical training collar known as a head halter. It's similar to the halter you would use for a horse. A strap goes behind the ears, a strap across the nose, and a ring under the chin where the leash attaches. The typical response to seeing a dog in a head halter is to ask, "Is that a muzzle?" You can assure whoever asks this that it's not in any way a muzzle. Your dog can open his mouth fully and eat and drink.

As usual, you will want to try out a few head halters to find out what is best for you and your dog. There are many different brands of head halters, so you'll have plenty to choose from.

Remember that the head halter, like the training collar, is a training tool. It should never be left on your dog unattended. Next, we will start discussing how to teach commands.

Chapter 5: taking command

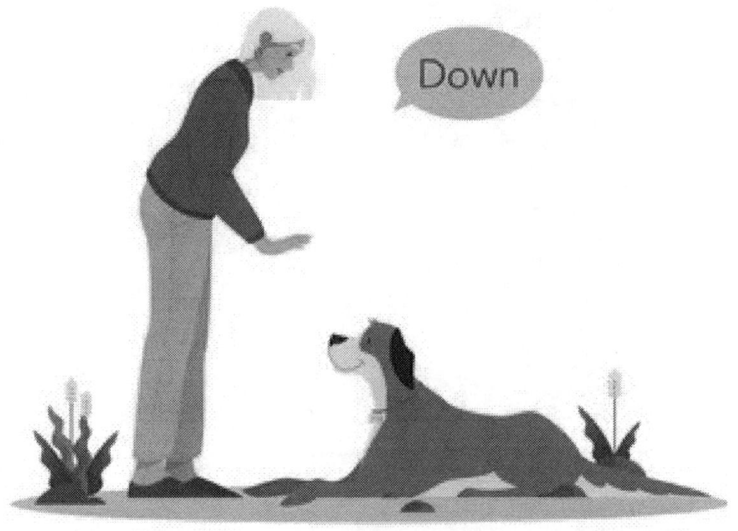

"With great power comes great responsibility." -uncle ben

Now that we've covered the different tools you can use for dog training, it's time to learn how to teach the actual commands. Here is where you must show that you are the pack leader of your super service dog pack and being a leader isn't a privilege; it's a responsibility. Always keep that in mind when teaching your dog new commands. You are the authority, so it is your responsibility to direct your dog properly. The command is defined as a verb that means "to direct with authority."

In the context of dog training, a command is a word or group of words you use when you want your dog to complete a specific action. Chances are your dog doesn't understand the language you speak, whether it's English, Spanish, French, mandarin, etc., but your dog will understand consistent communication. You might have even taught your dog several words in your language simply through positive reinforcement and repetition.

Now you will deliberately teach your dog the commands you want him to learn. These will also be learned through positive reinforcement and repetition, but the learning won't be incidental this time. You will be choosing specific words to convey specific meanings. You must be consistent in their usage if you want your dog to come to understand what they mean.

For your command words, you want to keep them as simple as possible and avoid making any of your command words sound similar to each other. Make them as distinct from each other as possible to avoid your dog thinking you mean one command when you mean a different one. Now we will talk about the tone of voice to use when giving commands.

There is a proper way to give a command assuming the person giving the command can speak and control their voice.

Otherwise, there isn't technically a proper way to give a command. Since this book is written with people with disabilities in mind, I will try to discuss the traditional way of giving verbal commands.

If you are fortunate enough to have a full range of vocal tones, you will want to make full use of your range when teaching commands to your dog. The tone of voice will communicate well your tone and thus your attitude and meaning. High pitch tones mean pleasure and approval. A firm and crisp tone means you are giving a command. A deep growl means disapproval. Try to use as much variation in your tone of voice as you can. This will give you more variety and range of how you communicate with your dog.

When we want someone to hear us, we tend to try to raise our voices. However, as you will learn from living with dogs, or as you may already know, dogs have perfect hearing. So your commands don't need to be loud. Soft is preferable. The loudness of your voice should only increase because you are doing so to add firmness to your voice for giving a command.

There are typically four parts to giving a command—name, command, praise, and release. Say your dog's name. Say the command word in a crisp tone. Praise your dog in a happy tone once he completes the task. Then release him with a word like "at ease," "easy," or "break." You will want to use a high pitch upbeat tone for the release word. Praise and a food reward should always come before you give the release word.

If you have difficulty speaking or forming words, you can still train your service dog. If you have some speech, your dog will be able to learn each distinct sound you make as a command. Other humans may not understand it, but your dog will. If you can make sounds but not words, the same rule applies. Your dog will be able to tell the subtle differences and sounds and recognize them as different commands. Again you want to be as consistent as possible and have one sound tied to the same action. If you can only make sounds, then varying the tone is even more important than usual.

Now, if you cannot make sounds, don't worry; you can still train your dog. As I stated earlier, dogs speak body language, which means they can understand signals. Smiles, frowns, hand gestures, etc., are all ways you can communicate with your dog if you can't make a sound on your own.

Again consistency is key for using signals to communicate with your dog. Be consistent with what signal goes with what command and make your signals distinct from each other. Now we can start learning specific commands and the first one we will start with is "attention."

Chapter 6: getting your dog's attention

"Attention is vitality. It connects you with others. It makes you eager. Stay eager."

-Susan Sontag

It should go without saying that to get your dog to do any of the tasks you want him to do, you have to be able to command your dog's attention. So the first exercise is getting your dog's attention. You will want to pick a word or short phrase to use when you want your dog to look at you. If you speak English, this word could be "look," "up," or even "attention." If you speak Spanish, you may say "Mira."

If you speak multiple languages or know a few words in another language, don't be afraid to use those as command words. Also, remember you can use sounds for commands. It's not uncommon for dog owners to make clicking sounds or whistling sounds to get their dog's attention.

Getting started - attention

Like any command, you will have to practice this until your dog has mastered it. Typically you will want to practice this command 2 to 3 times a day until your dog consistently looks at you on command. When you start teaching this command, you will want to be in a quiet place with no distractions. Have a lot of small food treats with you. Refer to chapter 2 to determine what best arrangement for giving food rewards works best for your situation.

To start, say your dog's name, followed by the attention command word. If you have a treat in hand that your dog can see, move it in front of your face. Your dog will likely follow the treat with his eyes. Once your dog looks at you, praise enthusiastically and give him the treat. Repeat this process over and over for about 2 minutes. Same sequence:

- Say name
- Say attention command
- Move the treat in front of the face
- Praise and give your dog the treat

Remember that if you have a friend help facilitate the training, make sure they wait until you have praised your dog before giving him the treat. Do what you have to to get your dog to look at you, and do not give praise or a treat before then. When using food as a training tool, you must be familiar with the concept of a "jackpot."

A jackpot is just what it sounds like, hitting a big pay-off all at once. In the case of dog training, it's a jackpot of treats. That is why I said earlier you want to have a lot of treats!

You want to use jackpots to solidify the positive reinforcement. If you are having your dog carry out the command in a problematic situation, it is a good idea to reward your dog with a jackpot if they successfully carry out the command. An example with the "attention" command would be your dog looking at you when you give the command, even if there are a lot of loud distractions around. That would be a perfect situation to give your dog a jackpot.

Intermediate stage - attention

When your dog looks at you quickly and consistently on command, you are ready to move on to the second stage of teaching attention. Now your dog will start to learn on his own what action brings the reward. Start off carrying out the exercise as usual. Have food ready, but don't say anything to your dog. He should recognize the situation and look at you readily. Praise "good look," "good attention," or "good [insert your command word]" and reward with a treat.

The next time your dog looks at you again, give enthusiastic praise and the food reward. If your dog doesn't look at you for about thirty seconds, give your "attention" command and praise when he looks. Anytime your dog looks at you without the "attention" command or signal, praise and reward your dog with a jackpot of treats. Remember to give praise and the food reward every time your dog looks at you.

Mastery stage - attention

Oncc your dog readily looks at you, you are ready to start having your dog master the "attention" command. This means working with distractions. The easiest thing to do is have a friend stand a few feet away and clap his hands to entice your dog. When you give your "attention," command your dog should look at you readily. If your dog is more interested in looking at your friend, then you will want to go back and practice the basics more.

If he ignores your friend and looks at you as he is supposed to, then give enthusiastic praise and reward your dog with a jackpot of treats. You will want to practice this several times. Each time try to make yourself more engaging to look at than your friend.

Don't stop practicing just because your dog has learned the "attention" command. This is something that will need to be constantly reinforced. The same is true for any command you teach your dog. The next command we will go over is the "sit" command.

Chapter 7: sit boy

"This is the magic secret of dog training -- lose control over yourself, and you at once lose control of the dog. Your strongest and the most irresistible weapon is iron patience."

-albert payson terhune

As you probably already know, the "sit" command is getting your dog to do just that, sit. This means your dog's bottom is on the floor. Every dog knows how to do this, but what you are doing is teaching your dog to sit when you tell him to. As always, you need to pick a word. Most people go with "sit" if they speak English or "senta" if they speak Spanish, but you don't need to feel restricted to that; just pick a word you will remember.

As with many of the basic commands, food is probably the best tool to get your dog to learn this command. However, as was stated earlier in chapter 2, some dogs have difficulty controlling themselves around food. “sit” is a good command to teach that can help get your dog more under control around food.

When teaching the "sit" command, hold a piece of food above your dog's head just out of reach. Don't hold it too high, or your dog will try to jump for it. Move the food treat slightly back over his head. As your dog watches the treat overhead, he will usually sink into the sit position. Be patient, as it might take a few minutes for your dog to do this. As soon as his bottom hits the floor, praise him by saying "good sit" and give him the food treat.

Remember, if you have speech difficulties, the same ideas apply here. Find a sound or signal you want to be the "sit" command. If holding the treat over your dog's head is something you aren't able to do, you can get a friend to do it for you, but again they can't give the food treat until after you've praised your dog for proper sitting.

You can also use feeding time as an opportunity to teach "sit." Just do the same thing you do with the food treat with your dog's food bowl, or have a friend do it if you can't hold the food bowl above your dog's head. When your dog sits, give them appropriate praise and place the food bowl in front of your dog. Remember always to give praise before the food.

Once your dog gets to the point where he readily sits, you are ready to have your dog master the "sit" command if you pull out food. Your dog's eagerness to sit when he sees you with a treat doesn't mean if he has thoroughly learned the "sit" command. It means he knows sitting is very likely going to get him a treat.

Get your dog on his feet and back away from him. He will follow you for the food. When your dog follows you, give your "sit" command. As soon as he sits, praise him. However, this time you want to wait at least 5 seconds before giving your dog the treat, then give the release command.

Practice this step several times for one week before you consider moving on. If your dog isn't sitting, go back to the first step of withholding the food over your dog's head. You will want to vary the amount of time between your dog following the "sit" command and getting the food reward but always praise as soon as he follows the command.

You want to randomize the amount of time between your dog following the command and getting the food because when you randomize rewarding a behavior, you strengthen the effects of the conditioning. Work on these varying lengths until you are confident your dog knows your “sit” command.

The best way to test if your dog has learned your "sit" command is to practice the exercise without food. Make sure your dog sees you don't have any food, and give the "sit" command and watch your dog's response. If you've been consistent with the command and giving praise, your dog should promptly respond to the command. If not, you need to take more time training the command.

When your dog is responding promptly, you can start doing the food reward less. However, do not eliminate the food reward. As stated earlier, randomizing when you give a positive reinforcer strengthens the conditioning of the desired behavior. Continue to practice the "sit" command as you move on to more advanced commands because you always want to reinforce the fundamentals. Next, we will go over a command similar to "sit" but distinctly different, and that is "down."

Chapter 8: down boy

"it is best to let sleeping dogs lie." -English proverb

When you have your service dog out in public, one thing you will have to account for is the fact that other people exist. Sometimes those people want to pet your dog. Sometimes they wish you didn't have a dog with you.

Sometimes they need to get around you and your dog, so you have to figure out the best way for you and your dog to move out of the person's way.

One command that is great for moving your dog out of the way of other people is the "down" command. It's just what it sounds like. Your dog lies down after you give this command. It doesn't matter if your dog lies on his back, side, or stomach. He just needs to be lying down. This may be one of the hardest commands to teach your dog because it is the most submissive position your dog can be in.

Getting started - down

There are a lot of different methods for teaching this command. You should decide which one works best for you and your dog. Make sure you are entirely prepared for the exercise before you even think about giving this command.

Meaning that your dog is on a leash, and you have plenty of food treats that are in easy reach.

For those who can reach down to the floor, this is the easiest method for teaching this command. With a piece of food in hand, put your hand just in front of your dog's nose and slowly move your hand outwards and downwards. His head will naturally follow your hand forward and down. Make sure you are moving your hand slowly and not jerking it to the floor.

As your dog's head moves down, give your "down" command and start praising with "good down" if you are able. Continue to move your hand slowly. Put your other hand on your dog's shoulder gently and encourage him to go down. Keep the food just out of reach, and be prepared for your dog to put his rear in the air as he goes down. This is a pretty common behavior for most dogs. Be patient, and just don't let him have the food until all his body is down.

The second your dog is down, immediately give praise followed by the food treat.

If reaching down to the floor is something you cannot do, the next best thing is to try to get your dog to your level. This could be done by having your dog come up on a couch. You may want to train them to do that on command first. Once you can get your dog up on a secure piece of furniture, you proceed the same way with teaching the command. Always remember to use your release command after you give praise and the food treat.

Intermediate stage - down

After you've practiced this repeatedly for two weeks, you should be ready to transition. If you used the first method, you would be working on getting your dog to go down on the floor after giving the command without following your hand for food. You can start by bending less and less when practicing the exercise. You will want to alternate the amount that you bend down. As soon as your dog goes down after you give the command, give the appropriate praise and move your hand down to the floor to give the food reward.

If you are using the second method, then the transition is a bit easier. Work on a sofa or some other secure piece of furniture for at least a week, consistently giving the down command followed by praise and the food reward. Then you can try practicing the exercise by sitting in a chair. If your dog has learned your "down" command, he should readily go down after you give it. You can move your hand with food in it closer to the floor, and as soon as your dog goes down, give the proper praise, then the food reward.

Mastery stage - down

Continue to practice the "sit" command and the "down" command several times each day, but don't always do them back to back after each other. Otherwise, your dog might build an association of expecting you to always give one command after the other. Your dog needs to learn each command distinctly. The next command we will teach is a dog training classic, the "stay" command.

Chapter 9: stay boy “be still.

Stillness reveals the secrets of eternity.” - Lao Tzu

M Any time in life, we have to take a deep breath, sit still, and gather our thoughts. Well, when you’re training a service dog, you will want your dog to be able to wait with you. That’s when the stay command can come in handy. Essentially the “stay” command is equivalent to “sit” or “down” but for a prolonged period. Specifically, until you give another command or release him, so your dog must master the “sit” and “down” commands before you can add this to the repertoire.

Getting started - stay

A good test to gauge your dog’s mastery is to give the “sit” and praise quietly when he sits and stay still and silently count to ten. If your dog moves within that time, you need to practice the "sit" command more. Do the same thing with the "down" command, and the same rule applies. If your dog stays still for a ten-second count, you're ready to teach "stay."

You will want to progress slowly with the "stay" command and not physically leave your dog when you first start teaching the command. The "stay" command can be tricky to teach your dog because the concept of doing nothing can be hard to communicate to a dog. When you start teaching this command, give the "sit" command and give appropriate praise.

Now give your dog your "stay" command. If you are physically able, you may want to add a hand signal to your "stay" command. For example, you can place your hand palm first flat in front of your dog's face to symbolize a barrier. As usual, you should figure out what works best for you and your dog. Don't move and quietly count to three. Quietly praise your "good stay", then release your dog.

Move around with your dog a bit, then repeat the exercise but this time, count to five. If your dog moves before a full five count, go back and practice the count to 3 several more times. Your dog likely has no concept of what he is doing correctly. That's why staying close, in the beginning, is important because you can be right there to correct your dog if he moves too soon.

Intermediate stage - stay

because you are trying to encourage stillness, praise should be quiet and not exuberant when teaching this command. Once you do hold the five-count after giving the "sit" command followed by the "stay" command, do the same thing with the down command. Command "down" and then give the "stay" command and do a silent three count. If your dog holds it, release him, walk around a bit, and repeat the exercise with a five-count.

If, for some reason, your dog seems to hold the "stay" command better with "sit" than "down" or vice versa, you can just teach "stay" from the preferred position. You should practice whichever command your dog won't stay for more until he becomes reliable with that command. Otherwise, alternating practicing "sit-stay" and "down-stay." Gradually increase the amount of time you have your dog in the "stay" position until you get to 1 minute.

Mastery stage - stay

Once your dog has gotten to this point, you can start practicing the exercise while leaving your dog. We will cover how to leave your dog in this exercise according to your level of mobility: ambulatory, ambulatory with devices, manual wheelchair, power chair.

Leaving your dog - ambulatory

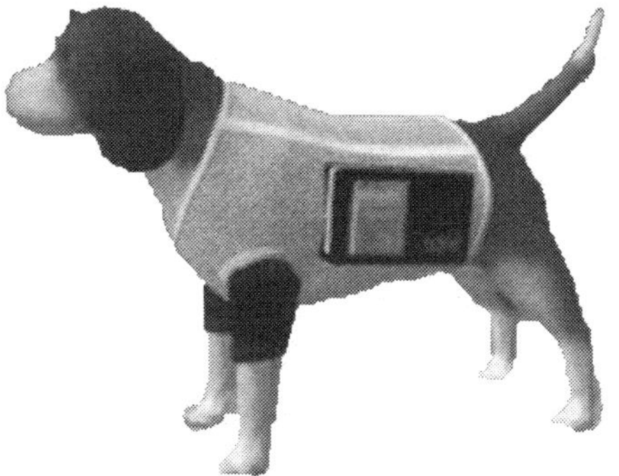

First, give your dog the "sit" command. Give the appropriate praise, then command "stay." Now take a small step away from your dog to the side. Then immediately step back beside him, praise quietly, then release. Walk around with your dog a bit and repeat the process. If your dog breaks before you give the release command, you need to spend more time working on the "stay" command while staying beside him.

Remember that patience is key if you need to practice "stay" without leaving your dog more than do so. As you are working on the "stay" command, gradually increase the amount of time you spend one step away from your dog until you get to 1 minute. Next, you will give the "sit" command, then the "stay" command, take the small step to the side, then step in front of your dog and turn to face him. It should just be a pivot in front of him, so you're right there, ready to make any needed correction if he starts to break. Quietly praise, "good stay" if your dog does not break, then pivot back beside him. Quietly praise again and then release.

Your dog should not break the stay when you return to his side or when he hears the praise. He should not move until he hears the release command. If your dog breaks before that, give a correction and get him back in position. Repeat your “stay” command, and leave him, but don’t step as far away and don’t step away for as long. When your dog is reliably consistent on this step, give your “stay” command, walk straight ahead four feet, turn and face him. Make sure that you don’t pull the leash tight as you walk away.

You can repeat the “stay” command when you face your dog. (this is where hand signals come in handy. You can use your signal as a reminder of the stay command.) Count to ten and then return to your dog’s side. Feel free to say the “stay” command again when you return besides your dog. If your dog did not break, stay, then praise quietly and give your release command. Always remember to alternate between practicing “stay” after the “sit” command and after the “down” command.

After this, all that is left to do is build up the time. You will want to practice “stay” in different locations and vary the length of time you have your dog stay. Be aware of your surroundings, and don’t practice the “stay” command in a place that would be a nuisance. For example, don’t have your dog go down in the middle of a busy doorway. So be aware of the possible circumstances that could arise when you pick locations to practice the “stay” command. Next, we will talk about how to teach this command if you are ambulatory with the help of devices.

Leaving your dog – ambulatory with devices

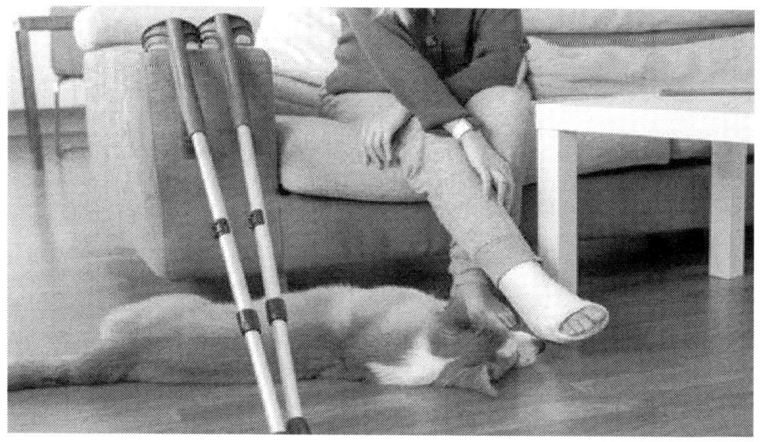

If you use canes, crutches, walkers, or any other device for mobility support, you will need to approach teaching “stay” with a bit more caution than if you were fully ambulatory. If you only use a device part of the time, you should still practice this exercise with your device so your dog will be used to it. This way, any distraction that could come about with having your devices, like dropping your cane, will be considered in the training.

In the case your cane or crutch falls on your dog, make sure to immediately express your sympathy in a high pitch and happy voice. Hopefully, your dog doesn't have a fear of your cane or crutch. If this is the case, refer back to chapter 3, where we discuss dealing with phobias.

When your dog is consistently staying for a minute, try practicing the exercise by dropping your crutch by you but away from your dog. It's best first to do this on a carpeted surface to minimize the amount of noise from the crutch dropping. You may want to sit in a chair as you practice this one not to lose your balance.

Give your "stay" command as you drop the crutch. Be prepared to repeat the command and correct your dog if needed. If your dog doesn't break the "stay," give your dog a lot of praise, then release. If he gets up, but goes back down on command, give appropriate praise, then release.

Next, practice the "sit" "stay" sequence three times without dropping your crutch.

Next, you will do the same exercise but use the "down" "stay" sequence. Give your dog your "down" command followed by your "stay" command as you drop your crutch. Again, be prepared to repeat the command and correct your dog if needed. Since down is the most submissive and vulnerable position a dog can take, don't be surprised if your dog is more prone to get up at the drop of the crutch in the down position than in the sit position.

Remember that patience is key. Make sure to practice having the crutch in front of and besides your dog. Don't move yourself, just the crutch, and make sure the crutch doesn't fall on your dog.

Your dog has to learn to be confident around the crutch and not to move once he hears the "stay" command regardless of what distraction there might be.

Once your dog ignores the falling crutch and reliably holds the "stay" position, you can start to move a step sideways away from your dog. First, give the "stay" command and take a step to the side away from your dog, then immediately step back and praise "good stay," then release. Walk around with your dog for a little bit, then repeat the sequence.

If your dog breaks, you need to spend more time working on the "stay" command while staying beside your dog. Remember not to rush. Haste makes waste because it's much harder to go back to square one than to do it right the first time. If your dog is reliably staying when you step away, then start to gradually increase the amount of time you step away until you get up to a minute.

Next, you will give the "sit" command, then the "stay" command, take the small step to the side, then step in front of your dog and turn to face him. It should just be a pivot in front of him, so you're right there, ready to make any needed correction if he starts to break. Quietly praise, “good stay” if your dog does not break, then pivot back beside him. Quietly praise again and then release.

Your dog should not break the stay when you return to his side or when he hears the praise. He should not move until he hears the release command. If your dog breaks before that, give a correction and get him back in position. Repeat your “stay” command, and leave him, but don’t step as far away and don’t step away for as long. When your dog is reliably consistent on this step, give your “stay” command, walk straight ahead four feet, turn and face him. Make sure that you don’t pull the leash tight as you walk away.

After this, all that is left to do is build up the time. You will want to practice “stay” in different locations and vary the length of time you have your dog stay. Be aware of your surroundings, and don’t practice the “stay” command in a place that would be a nuisance. For example, don’t have your dog go down in the middle of a busy doorway. So be aware of the possible circumstances that could arise when you pick locations to practice the "stay" command. Next, we will talk about how to teach this command if you are in a manual wheelchair.

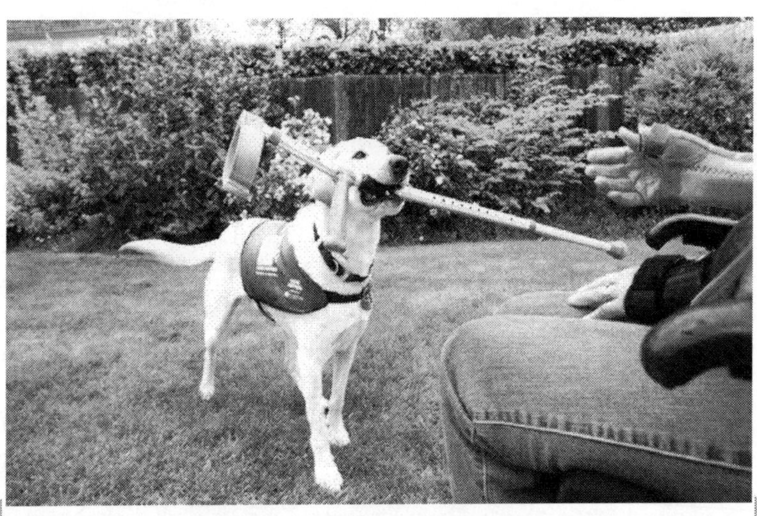

Leaving your dog - manual wheelchair

Your dog is most likely used to going beside you when you roll your chair and get out of the way of your chair. This is why the "stay" command can be more difficult to teach from a wheelchair. It can't be stated enough, so I'll repeat it. Patience is key, and if you are teaching "stay" from a wheelchair, you will need a lot of patience. Whenever you accidentally roll over your dog, you must immediately express your sympathy in a high pitched happy voice.

To start, give your "sit" command. Give your dog the appropriate praise, then give your "stay" command. Check your dog's position before you touch your wheels. If your dog is too close for you to move, give your release command, re-adjust and try again. Make sure there is no contact between your wheelchair and your dog.

When your dog is positioned so that you won't run into him with your chair, give your "stay" command, and move your chair forward just by a small amount of angling away from your dog.

You will barely move, and then you will roll back beside your dog and quietly praise, "good stay," then release him. Move around with your dog for a bit, then repeat the sequence. If your dog breaks before you give the release command, you need to spend more time working on the "stay" command while staying beside him. If your dog is holding the stay position reliably, start increasing the amount of time you move away until you get up to one minute.

Next, you will repeat the sequence, but you will roll about a foot away angled away from your dog this time.

Immediately roll back and quietly praise, "good stay," then release him. He should not move until he hears the release command. If your dog breaks before that, give a correction and get him back in position. Repeat your "stay" command, and roll away from him again, but don't move as far away and don't stay away for as long.

Start to gradually increase the time you have your dog hold the "stay" position. If you take your time and don't rush, each step will occur more quickly. Your dog is learning what you want, so remember to praise using "good stay" while you are away from your dog.

Next, you will repeat the "sit" "stay" command sequence, and this time you will move 4 feet away and turn your chair at a right angle towards your dog. Make sure the leash doesn't pull tight as you roll away. Feel free to repeat your "stay" command/signal when you face your dog. (this is where hand signals come in handy. You can use your signal as a reminder of the stay command.)

Count to ten to yourself, and return to your dog's side. Again, feel free to repeat your "stay" command/signal. Quietly give appropriate praise and release. If your dog shifted positions to avoid your wheel, but didn't move out of the sit position, give the command sequence again as a reminder and praise with "good stay." Next, give the "sit" "stay" command sequence to your dog, go forward at least 4 feet and turn to face your dog.

Make sure that if your wheelchair has footrests, they aren't hit your dog as you turn around. This is why you first practice this exercise at a right angle. Again make sure your leash never pulls too tight when you are moving away from your dog.

This is an example of where it is good to have multiple leashes at your disposal. A Flexi-leash might be the best to avoid pulling too tightly.

At each of these stages, make sure to alternate between practicing "sit", "stay", and "down" "stay." When your dog is reliably holding the "stay" position when you turn to face him, you can begin to gradually increase the time that you leave him in this position. As stated earlier, make sure to practice in different locations in addition to varying the time length. Next, we will discuss teaching "stay" from a power chair.

Leaving your dog - power chair

If you are using a power chair, your dog is most likely used to moving every time you click the motor of your chair. He anticipates either to go beside you, or he needs to get out of the way. Like in a manual wheelchair, this cueing can make teaching "stay" from a power chair more difficult. But as always, if you have patience, you will be able to overcome this added difficulty. Whenever you accidentally roll over your dog, you must immediately express your sympathy in a high pitched happy voice.

To start, give your "sit" command. Give your dog the appropriate praise, then give your "stay" command. Check your dog's position before you touch your controls. If your dog is too close for you to move, give your release command, readjust and try again. Make sure there is no contact between your wheelchair and your dog.

When your dog is positioned so that you won't run into him with your chair, give your "stay" command, and click your controls to make the motor noise but don't move yet because the motor noise is enough of a distraction for your dog to break the stay position.

Repeat the “stay” command as you click the motor, and quietly praise “good stay,” then release your dog. This step could take a few tries in the day or a few tries over a few weeks. Remember not to rush and go at the pace that works for your dog. You have to continue this step until there is no response from your dog when you click the motor. Remember that at this point, you have not moved away from your dog yet.

When your dog has learned to not move at the sound of the motor after you give the “stay” command, you will then be ready to practice the exercise by moving away from your dog. Go only 1 or 2 inches to start. Make sure you go forward angled away from your dog. Once you move forward a couple of inches, immediately move back, repeat the “stay” command, then praise, “good stay.”

Keep practicing until you can move away those few inches for up to a minute without your dog breaking the stay position.

Again, this could take up to a few weeks of practice for your dog to hold the stay position reliably. Gradually increase the amount of time. If you don't rush, you will see each step is learned more quickly. Your dog is learning what you want, so remember to praise using "good stay" while you are away from your dog.

Next, you will repeat the "sit" "stay" command sequence, and this time you will move 4 feet away and turn your chair at a right angle towards your dog. Make sure the leash doesn't pull tight as you roll away. Feel free to repeat your "stay" command/signal when you face your dog. (this is where hand signals come in handy. You can use your signal as a reminder of the stay command.)

If your dog shifted positions to avoid your wheel, but didn't move out of the sit position, give the command sequence again as a reminder and praise with "good stay." Next, give the "sit" "stay" command sequence to your dog, go forward at least 4 feet and turn to face your dog.

Make sure that if your wheelchair has footrests, they aren't hit your dog as you turn around. This is why you first practice this exercise at a right angle. Again make sure your leash never pulls too tight when you are moving away from your dog.

This is an example of where it is good to have multiple leashes at your disposal. A Flexi-leash might be the best to avoid pulling too tightly.

At each of these stages, make sure to alternate between practicing "sit" "stay" and "down" "stay." When your dog is reliably holding the "stay" position when you turn to face him, you can begin to gradually increase the time that you leave him in this position. As stated earlier, make sure to practice in different locations in addition to varying the time length. The next command we will learn to teach is "stand.

Chapter 10: stand

"Everything is a learning process: any time you fall over, it's just teaching you to stand up the next time." -Joel Edgerton

Hopefully, 'stand' means standing on all fours. And your dog does this all the time, but what you want to do is teach your dog to stand on command and hold the position for as long as you need it. There is a command that has your dog get on his back feet and put his front paws up onto something, but we cover that command in volume 2.

You might not see any particular reason for the "stand" command, but it can be a beneficial exercise. If you groom your dog yourself, having him stand still while you brush him might be helpful. This also makes it easier for a veterinarian to do an examination.

another useful command to teach a service dog is "brace." This is where your dog allows you to gently lean on him so you can get up from a chair or the floor, and of course, the "stand" command is a prerequisite for this. We cover the "brace" command in more detail in volume 2.

Getting started - stand

Although standing is one of the things your dog does the most, teaching your dog to stand in one position on command for an extended period may take some time. Again patience will be your greatest asset. Since your dog has learned to sit on command, and he knows sitting can get him a treat, you may have to do a lot of correcting if your dog is quick to sit as you are practicing the "stand" command.

There are a few methods for teaching "stand," As always, you should experiment to see which method will work best for you and your dog. The key is to get your dog off his bottom. You can try to walk him forward a few steps and give your "stand" command. As soon as you stop moving, he is likely to try to sit. If possible, slip your hand under his belly, just in front of his back legs, to gently prevent him from sitting while you say, "good stand." Wait only about 2 seconds, remove your hand and release him.

If you have difficulty moving forward, you can hold a piece of food in front of your dog's nose and move it straight out away from him. Don't raise it, or he will sit for it. Move it out in a straight line from his nose. As he stands up to follow the food, say your dog's name and "stand." Praise, "good stand," and give him the treat while he's standing, then quickly release.

It will probably be best to have your dog up on a raised surface if you can't bend over, just like with the down command.

Once he is on a sofa or another stable piece of furniture, use food to entice him to stand and place your hand gently under his flank. Say your dog's name and the "stand" command, and praise "good stand" while he is standing. Give the release command after a few seconds.

Regardless of the method you decide to use, remember that your dog does not know what you're asking him to do first. So you must be consistent. Make sure to praise him as soon as possible; otherwise, you might praise him when he tries to sit back down.

Practice this exercise faithfully for at least a week. He should be starting to get the idea of what the "stand" command means.

Now give your "stand" command and see how your dog responds. If he starts to get up, encourage and praise him. Hold a treat out in front of him to show him the position you want. If he doesn't move at all, then continue to practice as you have been. Your dog just needs more time. Make sure you give the command and make sure you praise when he's in the correct position.

You are trying to do many things at once, and you need to concentrate on doing them properly for your dog to learn this command. If you tug up on the leash, your dog will probably sit, so make sure any leash movement is straightforward. If you raise your hand holding the treat, your dog will probably sit, and if you lower your hand, he will most likely lie down. So you will need to keep your hand on a straight line out from his nose.

Remember to give your "stand" command so your dog can associate the word with this action and praise "good stand." Make sure you give the command and the praise as your dog is standing, not when he's about to sit. Wait no more than two seconds before you give your release command. Again patience is key. This will take a week or two of consistent practice for your dog to learn the specific meaning of your "stand" command. And it can take months for your dog to understand it thoroughly and follow it promptly.

Intermediate stage - stand

You will want to practice the "stand" command regularly. Gradually increase the time you ask your dog to remain in the stand position. Put your hand gently under his belly, if you are able, as a reminder to stay on all fours. Praise quietly and gently stroke his belly. Wait several seconds, as you tell him "good stand," then release him.

Sometimes, instead of releasing him, you can try to give him another command like sit or down, but make sure to praise after obeying each command. When your dog readily obeys the "stand" command, take your hand away from under his belly. Keep praising "good stand," so he understands he's supposed to remain in that position.

If he sits when you take your hand away, he doesn't know the "stand" command yet, and you need to practice more. If he holds the stand position, give him the appropriate praise, then release him. Now, give your "stand" command. Praise when he stands. Next, give your "stay" command just as you did with "sit" and "down." If you have a hand signal for "stay," use it in front of your dog's face to remind him of the meaning of the "stay" command.

If your dog moves to sit down, correct him by saying something like "uh-uh-uh" or "no" and repeat "stand, stay." After a couple of seconds, praise and release. At this point, all that is left is to build up time on the “stand stay” sequence just as you did for “sit” and “down.” The only difference is you don’t have to worry about moving away from your dog since most if not all the times you will need to use the command, you will be right by your dog.

Mastery stage - stand

When your dog holds the “stand, stay” position for at least thirty seconds, have a friend come up and pet him while he holds the position. If he moves to greet the person, give a verbal correction and a firm reminder that your dog’s on a stand and a stay command. Have your friend move back as you reposition your dog, then try again.

Again this may take quite a few tries, but he will eventually learn to hold the “stand, stay” position even when touching him. This will be very helpful for the veterinarian. It’s good to practice this exercise with as many different people as possible. If your dog is shy, make sure they are people your dog knows and likes. I would recommend practicing this command several times before taking your dog to the veterinarian. Remember to work with lots of praise and treats. The next exercise we will go over is known as “random recall,” which is simply getting your dog to come to you whenever you call.

Chapter 11: random recall

"dogs are loyal, patient, fearless, forgiving, and capable of pure love. Virtues that few people get through life without abandoning, at least once." -m.k. Clinton

Among humans, dogs have garnered quite the reputation of loyalty. A loyal friend is always there when you need them, and your super service dogs will be no different. However, you will want to train your dog to come

whenever you call him. In other words, you want your dog to be able to be recalled at random.

Thus, we call this exercise random recall.

For your dog to learn that coming to you when you call takes top priority over any distractions, you will need always to praise and reward your dog when he comes to you. In addition, if you are calling your dog to do something he isn't a fan of, like grooming, you need to praise your dog first before grooming so that coming to you is always followed first by something positive. It's important to remember that this recall is not to be done using the "come" command if you can't enforce the command.

getting started - random recall

Food will be the primary motivator for teaching random recall. You are going to use the dog's instinct to go towards food. Always praise enthusiastically every time he follows the command. You can start by using feeding time as a training tool.

As you go to the room where your dog eats, say his name and "come" in a happy voice. As you get the food, even though he's right there with you, say his name and "come" in a happy voice. As soon as your dog looks at you, give praise.

This is not a command; you are just building a positive association with the word you will use as the command. Do this for at least a week. Say his name and "come" using a high-pitched, happy voice every time you feed your dog. At some point when your dog is sleeping, you will want to try the recall command where he eats when he isn't there. Rattle the food bag or box and call him.

Use a high-pitched, happy voice to say his name and "come." He should come running. Give enthusiastic praise and the food treat. If you can't sneak away from your dog, then have a friendly pet and distract him while you go to where your dog eats to give the command. The second you call your dog, your friend has to immediately release your dog so he can come to you asap!

You want to ensure you have control of your dog when he comes, so give your "sit" command when he gets to you. You don't want your dog to think that he can run on past you. Decide if you want your dog to sit in front of you or to one side or the other. After you decide where the best spot is, use the food to get your dog there. As soon as he comes to you, praise for the recall, but move your hand with the food treat to the place where you want him to go. As soon as he's there, give your "sit" command, give the appropriate praise, and give the food treat as soon as your dog sits.

It's a good idea to make this a regular part of your recall training. Remember to always praise separately for the recall and the sit. So you will sometimes want to have at least two food treats in hand.

Practice this for at least one week, then give the command from a different room. Remember to use a high-pitched, happy voice.

Praise your dog as he's coming to you and as soon as he comes to you, give the food treat. Then have him move to the designated spot to sit.

intermediate stage - random recall

Dog's enjoy hide and seek, so this will be good bonding for you and your dog. As with everything in dog training, "slow is fast", so you want to increase the difficulty of finding yourself gradually. When you first start, keep it easy for your dog to find you. Then slowly make it more difficult to find you. Always call and encourage your dog the entire time he is searching for and coming to you.

Before you know it, your dog will come running whenever you call him. It's important to keep this a positive and happy experience because you are training a super service dog that doesn't even need to think about whether or not he will respond to your recall command. It should be such a positive association that is simply hearing the "come" command causes an automatic response.

When your dog gets to this point, you can start to taper off with the food rewards. You can start to leave out the food reward every fourth recall, then every third, you can randomize the food reward. However, remember always to give praise even when you are tapering off with the food rewards.

Mastery stage - random recall

Now it's time to start mastering the random recall. This is going to require you to practice in different locations. If you have a fenced backyard, that is a good place to start. Treat it like you are beginning a new exercise, so give food every time, at least for a week. When starting, it's best to have a quiet environment with no distractions.

When you are in the backyard, as soon as your dog starts to move away from you, say his name and your "come" command in a happy tone of voice. If your dog doesn't come, that means he doesn't know what you want, and you should go practice inside more. If your dog does come, give enthusiastic praise and a food reward. You may have to remind your dog where he is supposed to sit. If needed, you use food to get him to his proper position and give enthusiastic praise before saying your release word. The next exercise we will cover is the controlled walk.

Chapter 12: the controlled walk

"All truly great thoughts are conceived while walking." - Friedrich Nietzsche

In obedience training terms, a person and dog walking together are called "heeling." This is a very formal and structured exercise with the person walking a certain way and the dog on the left side in a "proper heel position." If you're thinking about entering obedience competitions, you will have to formally learn to do this exercise. But to talk your dog out in public, you simply need to learn how to perform the “controlled walk.”

A controlled walk is when your dog is walking beside you with slack on the leash. If he is pulling, weaving, or sniffing the ground all the time, he may be walking, but he is not controlled. You want to get your dog to learn to walk at your side calmly and at your pace. This means your dog stops when you stop and turns when you turn.

Getting started - heel

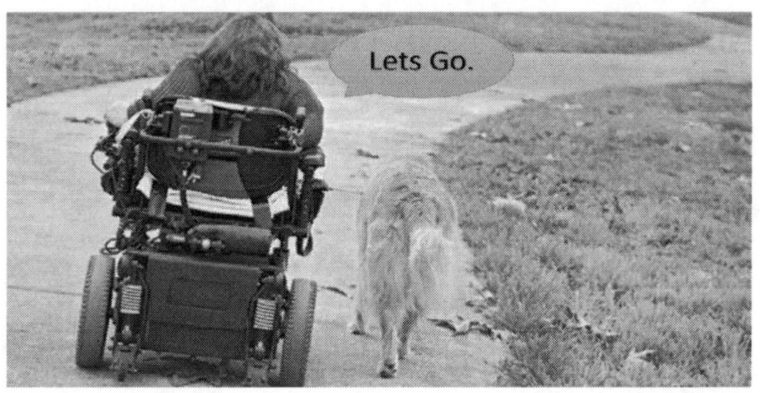

Dogs naturally like to move quickly, so if you are in a wheelchair or power chair, this could be to your advantage, but don't worry if you move more slowly. Your dog will learn to adjust. There are three parts to a controlled walk. You are starting, walking, and stopping. You will need to practice and master all three to achieve a well-controlled walk.

When starting, you want to give your command to begin the controlled walk. Traditionally this command is "heel", but as always, you can use whatever word or phrase you like. “let’s go,” “walk,” “caminar” are all words and phrases that you can use.

Whatever phrase you choose, remember always to give the command as you begin to move. Don’t start to move and then say “heel.” Even though dogs are in tune with human emotion, the chances are your dog can’t read your mind, so your dog needs to be told whether you expect him to stay or to move with you.

You always want to have a goal of starting the controlled walk as smoothly as possible. You then proceed at your own pace, and your dog should make adjustments based on your pace. Your dog will learn to pay attention to you so that he knows to turn when you turn. He will learn to walk close enough to you so that his leash doesn't get caught on anything, but not so close that he crowds you. Talk to your dog to keep his attention and praise “good heel.” You must keep a happy tone of voice during this exercise

Whenever you stop, your dog needs to stop as well immediately. If you want your dog to start sitting whenever you stop, give him your “sit” command every time you stop. If you rather your dog stand, give a “wait” or “stop” command instead. The most important thing is that your dog stops next to you and awaits your next command.

When you first start teaching the controlled walk, this is the first time you are asking your dog to move along beside you. You started by teaching your dog the control commands like “sit,” “down,” “stand,” and “stay.” Next, you taught your dog to come to you whenever you called. Now you must teach your dog to move with you at your pace. You shouldn't expect your dog to understand what you're asking of him first; start practicing in a quiet area with no distractions. You want to aim to build up positives and set your dog up for success. So it's best to begin teaching your "heel" command in an area where you will have your dog's undivided attention. If you alternate between walking and using a wheelchair, you will want to practice the "heel" exercise both ways. Your pace in a wheelchair will be different from your average walking pace, and you'll need to help your dog learn to make the necessary adjustments between the two.

If you have better control from the wheelchair, you may want to consider starting that way. When your dog learns what heel means, and he's walking beside you under good control, you can practice on foot. Only walk short distances when you start practicing. Your dog won't innately know what position or pace you want, so you will have to teach him. This means you don't give in to going at your dog's pace. You teach your dog to adjust to yours.

Before moving, say your dog's name followed by your "heel" command, then move forward. If he doesn't immediately move with you, give a light tug on the leash and repeat the command if your dog leaps ahead of you, command him to stop and sit. Praise for the stop. Repeat your heel command and move forward again. Don't be surprised if it takes a lot of starts and stops before your dog understands what you want.

Your dog will get tired of the constant stopping and sitting and ultimately move under more restraint. When he finally decides to walk beside you, praise "good heel." Do this even if it's only a few steps. If he then decides to jump ahead again, stop and command him to stop and sit. You want to correct the behavior you don't want (i.e., Leaping ahead), and you want to praise for the behavior you want (i.e., Walking next to you at your pace).

Intermediate stage - heel

As with all commands, patience and consistency are the keys to success. If you are using a traditional training collar, you must use it correctly in heeling. If it's tight all of the time, you aren't communicating correctly with your dog. You have to give a "jerk and release", as explained in chapter 4. If you're using a head halter, just remember to give slack when your dog is in the proper position.

Now, if you have the opposite problem of your dog lagging behind you, you can hold a piece of food while moving. You'll probably find this helpful if your dog is lagging. If you can't hold food during the walk, you will have to make your praise enough of a reward. Start with concise sessions of straight-line heeling. Keep your tone of voice happy and light, but praise with a lot of enthusiasm every time your dog properly walks beside you at your pace. As always, patience is key for a dog who lags behind you.

If you want to carry out a controlled walk with your dog successfully, you need to decide the correct position for your dog when walking with you. It should ultimately be based on what works best for you. Remember that with walking devices and wheelchairs, your dog will naturally heel wider beside the walking devices or wheelchair. It's up to you to choose the best position for your dog. Don't let your dog wander; whether you are wandering ahead of you or behind you, you want to correct your dog whenever he is out of position.

Remember, if you are using a walking device or a wheelchair, make sure the leash does not get tangled. This could result in your dog receiving an unfair correction, and again consistency is one of the keys to successful dog training. There should only be enough slack in the leash for your dog to walk in the place you have decided as the "heel position."

You may want to mark the leash where you want to hold it just to be as consistent with this exercise as possible. When in a manual wheelchair, make sure you have enough slack in the leash to do a backward stroke with your wheelchair, but not so much that the leash will get tangled in the whcel.

After you've practiced numerous sessions of short, straight-line heeling, you'll want to begin practicing turning and moving around obstacles. This will help your dog to learn to pay attention to you while walking. Communication is key. You want to be talking to your dog. Tell your dog when you are going to turn. This can be where hand signals come in well...handy. When turning, you don't want it to be an abrupt rigid turn. Gradual and easy changes in direction are best. You may want to use commands like "right" or "left." Again, hand signals or any other kind of signals can be very useful with this exercise. Give your dog plenty of warning before you turn.

If you use crutches or any other walking device, they can be helpful to training tools as long as they are used gently. When you get ready to turn, you can put the crutch in front of your dog if he's too far ahead of you. Praise immediately when he moves back beside you. You can push lightly with the crutch if your dog is crowding you too much. Just make sure you don't use your walking device in such a way that you make your dog afraid of it.

Practicing turns from a manual or power wheelchair can give you a tremendous advantage when doing this exercise. The chair itself can be used as a training tool. To teach your dog to watch you, turn quickly in either direction. As always, be careful not to run over your dog. Your dog will soon learn to pay attention when walking beside you if the wheelchair comes at him all of a sudden or spins away from him.

Mastery stage - heel

After numerous short sessions, you and your dog should be able to do the controlled walk fairly well. Now it's time to work on perfecting it. It can't be overstated how important patience and consistency are when practicing this exercise. If you aren't consistent with what you expect from your dog, he will get sloppy.

Whenever you give your "heel" command, your dog must remain in the heel position until you give him your release command.

When your dog is under your "heel" command, he should not go to greet other dogs or people. This is extremely important when you are walking in crowded areas filled with people like a mall. If you will release your dog to let him visit with another dog or person, make sure your dog is under control before giving the release command. It's best to work in a quiet park initially, and then you can work your way to a more crowded park.

If you want to let your dog run and play in a dog park, make sure you keep your dog under control until you get to the enclosure.

Have your dog heel up to the fence, and if your dog isn't doing heal properly, turn around and continue to practice heel. The goal is to get your dog to pay attention to you regardless of all the distractions your dog wants to engage in. It's critical to take your time to build up your dog's confidence as well as composure. The next command we will go over is probably one of the simplest to understand but one of the most important commands for your dog to learn. And that command is the "wait" command.

Chapter 13: time to wait

"patience is not simply the ability to wait – it's how we behave while we're waiting."

-Joyce Meyer

One question you might be asking is, "what makes 'wait' any different from 'stay'?" The difference is the expectation you set for your dog. With the "stay" command, you expect your dog to hold the same position until you give another command.

This is not the case with the "wait" command. For example, you probably aren't expect your dog to remain completely motionless in your home when you leave your dog at home.

Getting started- wait

Despite this, many people will give their "stay" command as they leave the house. However, they don't mean for their dog to "stay" regarding what the command means. So it is essential to know exactly what each of your commands means so you don't confuse your dog. When you give your "wait" command, you tell your dog that there is a specific area he isn't supposed to cross until you give another command.

Imagine that you have built an invisible barrier your dog is to wait behind until you return. You will want to teach your dog that things like doors, gates, fences, etc., serve as "wait barriers." Your dog will eventually learn to wait for your permission. Opening a door or gate will not mean your dog has carte blanche to go through whatever door or gate. Just like random recall, the "wait" command can be a lifesaver. Just as the random recall will have your dog return to you if he is about to wander off into somewhere dangerous, the "wait" command can prevent your dog from wandering off into the dangerous place altogether.

As stated earlier, the "wait" command is probably the most straightforward command to understand and yet one of the most crucial commands for your dog to learn. Fortunately, the command is not only easy to understand, but it is easy to teach as well. However, patience and consistency are still key to maintaining. This means if you have been letting your dog run out the door or jump out of the car, you have to decide that you will no longer allow your dog to do this, and he has to learn to wait for permission. Being consistent means your dog has to wait every time a "wait barrier" is opened.

This means you can't allow your dog to slip away when you open a door. To do this, you have to have control over the different situations. Don't open your front door unless your dog is on a leash and by your side. Remember, dogs have excellent hearing. So you shouldn't assume your dog won't hear you open the door if he's in another room.

Your dog could come bolting out of the other room and out the door, and if this happens, he just got rewarded for incorrect behavior. This means you shouldn't try to give your "wait" command unless you know you can keep him from bolting out the door.

When practicing to teach your dog to wait at an open door, put your dog on a leash and give your "wait" command before you open the door. You want to start with opening the door only slightly or have a friend do it if you need assistance with this exercise. Give your "wait" command, then shut the door or "wait for barrier" firmly. If your dog backs away when you shut the door, praise "good wait."

Next, repeat the sequence, but open the door a bit more this time. If your dog tries to exit through the larger opening, use the leash to stop him. If you're in a wheelchair, the wheelchair can be used as well to keep your dog from leaving. Make sure you don't close the door on your dog's head and be sure to praise enthusiastically when he backs up.

Most dogs aren't fond of a door being slammed in their face, so this technique gets your dog to learn the command pretty quickly. Do this exercise several times a day for several days, at least a week. You will begin to see your dog backing up as you give your "wait" command. Your dog isn't going to want to wait for you to slam the door before backing up. This means your dog is learning what your "wait" command means.

Now you are ready to try opening the door all the way. Remember to give your "wait" command before you open the door. Have your dog on a leash next to you and go up to the doorway. Stop wherever you decide you want the "wait barrier" to be. Typically, it's the doorjamb that you don't want your dog to cross without permission. Once you reach the "wait for barrier", give your "wait" command again. Make sure to use a firm tone of voice or give an emphatic signal to show your dog you are serious about this command.

If your dog backs up or even just stops, praise “good wait.” If he tries to go out the door, stop him by using the leash. Again, if you are in a wheelchair, you can usc the wheelchair to block your dog from exiting out the door. If you are struggling with this step, you should spend more time on the previous steps to open the door then shut it firmly. Keep practicing that step until your dog unequivocally responds to your “wait” command and not the door slamming. You also want to be aware of any distractions that might be outside when you approach the open door. In the beginning, you want distractions to be at a minimum. You can add in distractions as your dog improves with the command.

The two things your dog needs to learn when at an open front door are as follows:

- Your dog must learn to wait and then go out with you on your command.
- Your dog must also learn that there are times when he will not be allowed to go out at all.

When your dog is obediently waiting beside you without trying to leave out the door, praise enthusiastically with "good wait." Then give your release command/signal or a command/signal to tell your dog to go outside. When practicing this exercise, you and your dog should always go out together, with your dog under control. If your dog has a habit of trying to leap out ahead of you, give him your "heel" command so he knows he hasn't been released yet.

If you're in a wheelchair, chances are you need him to get behind you to get through the door. You can use a "back" or "behind" command to instruct your dog to position himself behind you. This will come in handy whenever you are in close quarters with your dog. As stated earlier, your dog will need to learn that there are times when he will not be allowed to go out at all. This means that your dog needs to know that there will be times when you go out the door, but your dog must not follow you and wait behind the door.

To teach this, when your dog is doing an excellent job of waiting beside you, repeat your "wait" command as you go through the doorway. Use your body to block your dog if he tries to leave. Again, if you have walking devices or a wheelchair, you can use those to block your dog from leaving as well. Give your "wait" command firmly, then praise "good wait." You should praise quietly so your dog doesn't interpret your praise as an invitation to follow you out the door.

You should go only a step or two outside of the door and then come right back beside your dog. Give appropriate praise and release your dog by moving away from the door into the house. Don't give your dog a chance to bolt out the door. You may need help with this part of the exercise, especially if you're in a wheelchair. This is because it's not easy to see what your dog is doing as you're going out the door unless you have eyes in the back of your head, which is probably not the case.

You can have a friend stand behind your dog and hold the leash. If your dog tries to follow you out the door, your friend will give a tug as you repeat your "wait" command. Gradually build up the time and distance that you can leave your dog waiting at the open door. Remember, if you allow your dog to run outside after you give your "wait" command, then you are letting him be rewarded for incorrect behavior, which will take longer to correct.

intermediate stage - wait

After at least a week of consistently practicing this stage of the exercise, you should be able to leave your dog with your "wait" command at an open door for at least several minutes. You can do things like getting things from your car or checking your mail without your dog running out the door.

Be aware that the amount of time needed for a dog to learn this exercise will vary wildly from dog to dog. If a dog has been allowed to run out of the door for years, naturally, it will take that dog longer to learn the "wait" command than a dog who isn't used to being allowed to run out of an open door. Either way, it can take up to multiple months before a dog has the "wait" command down perfectly. Remember, if you have multiple entryways to in and out of the house, you should teach your dog to follow the "wait" command at every "wait barrier." For example, if you have a front gate in your front yard, you should train yourself to wait behind the gate and your front door.

When you move to a new "wait barrier," you should treat it as a new exercise. So, you will start practicing the wait command from the very beginning when you are at a new "wait barrier." Your dog will learn more quickly each time you reach a new “wait barrier.” However, you should always give your “wait” command whenever the door is opened, no matter how obedient your dog has become while waiting at an open door or gate.

Even when your dog is in another room away from the door, get into the habit of giving your “wait” command every time you open the door. Also, when you return to your house, give the “wait” command firmly as you open the door. Again, do this even if your dog is in another room away from the door. Next, we will talk about getting your dog to wait in the car.

Mastery stage - wait

Most dogs are extremely eager to arrive anywhere, and if you are driving, as soon as the car is parked, your dog will probably want to get out asap. So, unless you teach your dog otherwise, he’s belting out the car door as soon as it’s open. However, the whole point of the "wait" command is to teach your dog to operate on your time, not his.

You have to teach your dog to wait for permission to leave the car. The safest way to transport a dog in the car is with a seat belt or in a crate. This way, your dog can't disturb you while you are driving. Additionally, your dog is much safer in the case of an accident, and a seat belt or crate makes teaching "wait" in the car a lot easier. However, if your dog rides loose in the car, you must train your dog to travel calmly and exit the car at your command.

If you are able, you can teach this in a very similar manner to how you taught your dog to wait at your front door. If your dog has the habit of bolting out of the first open car door, give your "wait" command in a firm voice before opening a car door. As you did before, start with only barely opening the door then closing it firmly. Give appropriate praise if your dog backs away by saying, "good wait." Next, repeat the sequence but open the door a little further. Make sure to give appropriate praise.

This stage might take numerous repetitions before your dog learns to wait for you to get out of the car first. Again, if you cannot practice this exercise unassisted, enlist the help of a friend to open and shut the car door as you give the "wait" command. To ensure your dog doesn't just leap out of the car at the first chance he gets, you may want to attach his leash to some fixed object in the car. However, your dog should never have a choke collar or head halter on when the car is moving. Nor should you attach the leash to an object in the car during movement. It's far too dangerous. Now we will go over how to teach your dog to leave objects he has found.

Chapter 14: leave it

"There are far, far better things ahead than any we leave bchind." -c.s. Lewis

We've all heard the saying, "curiosity killed the cat," but don't get the wrong idea. Dogs are just as curious, if not more curious, than cats. Now, curiosity is a healthy emotion that can help us learn new things, but just like a child, curiosity combined with a lack of knowledge can be very dangerous.

Your dog isn't always going to know if something he wants to touch or sniff is safe to touch or not. When your dog is interested in an object he needs to leave alone, it's your responsibility to give your dog a command that tells him to leave the object of interest alone. That is the purpose of the "leave it" command. Food on the ground will probably be the biggest temptation for your dog, but with diligent and consistent training, your dog can learn never to eat any food off the ground.

Getting started - leave it

As usual, it doesn't matter the word or phrase you use for this command as long as you can remember and are consistent with how you use it; any word or phrase will work for this exercise.

Again, if you can't form words, then find a deep gruff sound you can make. This command should not be given in a happy tone. It needs to have a deep and firm tone. If you can't make any sound on your own, find a signal you can use. The signal should be sharp and abrupt.

When you start teaching this command, try using a food item your dog doesn't find very tempting. As your dog becomes more reliable with this command, you can move to more enticing food. An exercise like this is easiest to teach with the help of a friend. Have your dog on a leash by your side.

Make sure you have a little bit of slack on the leash, but not much. Now have your friend put a small piece of food a couple of feet in front of you. As your friend places the food on the ground before you, give your "leave it" command. If your dog moves towards the food, use the leash to stop him and firmly repeat your "leave it" command.

If your dog is wearing a training collar, use the "jerk and release" method discussed in chapter 4. Do not keep the leash tight. Give your dog slack and make the necessary correction. If you're using a head halter, loosen the leash as soon as he stops pulling toward the food. If you are in a wheelchair, you can use it to prevent your dog from getting the food. When you use the chair to block your dog, repeat your "leave it" command firmly.

Your dog mustn't get to the food. Otherwise, he is being rewarded for inappropriate behavior. So, you must be completely ready to make any needed corrections for this exercise before the food is placed on the ground. If you aren't ready, it's best not to give the command at all as not to confuse your dog.

When your dog looks away from the food or puts slack on the leash, praise "good leave it."

Your dog may very well try to move toward the food again. Be ready to repeat the command firmly and make a leash correction if needed, and give appropriate praise when he backs off. When you do this, only leave the food on the ground for a few seconds. Long enough for him to put slack in the leash so you can give praise. Your friend should then pick up the food and put it out of reach. Never give this piece of food as a reward to your dog for obeying the "leave it" command. You can set it aside and use it as a reward for a different exercise if you want. But your dog must understand that "leave it" means he doesn't get the food.

Only practice this exercise once per training session. This is because you want to build up this exercise slowly. Work on "leave it" two or three times a day with the food placed 2 feet away.

Slowly increase the time that you leave the food on the ground. Do this based on your dog's reaction. If you have a dog used to eating everything he finds on the floor, then this step could take up to several weeks. Again, patience and consistency are key.

When your dog stops fighting the leash to get the food, start having your friend place the food item only 1 foot away. Give a firm "leave it" command, and be ready to make any needed corrections. Give praise when your dog allows slack in the leash.

Then use your "attention" command /signal to get your dog to look at you. Give very enthusiastic praise when he does.

This is the best response to your “leave it” command. Your dog turns away from food to look at you. If your dog doesn’t look at you, move away from the food with him and get his attention on you. Then give appropriate praise.

This command is essential for your dog to learn, so you want to make sure your dog responds consistently. This means practicing under controlled conditions as often as you can before testing your dog when you don’t have leash control. Most dogs will hear the disapproval in your voice if you give the command properly.

Because your dog wants to please you, hearing the disapproval encourages the dog to overcome his natural desire for the food. So, make sure you give the command firmly every time and always remember to give appropriate praise as soon as your dog turns away from the food or stops pulling forward.

As with all commands, you don't want to shout your "leave it" command. You want to give your dog quiet-but-firm commands. You probably don't want to call attention to yourself by shouting at your dog. Practice for at least one week, two to three times a day, with the food item only one foot away from your dog.

Consider varying the kind of food you use from not that enticing to very enticing. Remember, don't give food as a reward for the "leave it" command.

Now place a piece of food on the floor and walk with your dog past it. Give your "leave it" command as you approach the food item, and prepare to make any needed corrections. If your dog lowers his head toward the food, firmly repeat your "leave it" command and quickly move away from the food. Give enthusiastic praise if your dog listens to your first "leave it" command.

Intermediate stage - leave it

You should practice this step for at least a week. If your dog is always pulling toward the food, then you might not be giving your command firmly enough. Also, check with all the other members of your household to make sure no one is giving your dog food without your permission. Make sure you praise your dog immediately and enthusiastically when he obeys your "leave it" command.

Keep in mind that you want your dog to obey your verbal “leave it” command or signal. Although you can make corrections with the leash, at times when your dog isn’t on a leash, this won’t be an option. So, you want to continue practicing this exercise until your dog obeys your command and not simply the leash correction. You want to get to the point where the leash corrections are no longer needed. Now, this can take a lot of time, but remember, patience is key.

Now, this might be obvious, but it’s worth stating that the “leave it” command isn’t just supposed to be used to get your dog to leave food. It can be used to get your dog to leave anything that has caught his attention. It can be your shoes or the neighbor’s cat. Whatever it is, your “leave it” command should be used in any situation where you want your dog to leave something alone. This is important because the “leave it” command will get your dog to ignore something that could be detrimental to your dog’s health.

Whether it is an item your dog could choke on or an item that could poison your dog.

It's also important to be aware of your dog's body language and posture because you can't constantly stare at your dog or monitor what is on the ground in front of your dog. However, once you are aware of your dog's body language, you will be able to instantly tell when he becomes more alert because something caught his attention. You'll likely see your dog's ears perk up, his body tenses up, or you feel a slight tug on the leash.

These signals will let you know your dog is interested in something he has seen before you even look to see what it is that has your dog's interest. And before you look to see what it is, you should give your "leave it" command, which will immediately cause your dog to turn away from whatever caught his attention. After he has mastered the "leave it" command, of course.

Mastery stage - leave it

Now the "leave it" command applies not only to items besides food but also to items located in other places besides the ground. Most of us have probably seen a dog grab food off of a table, and these are exactly the kind of things a well-mannered super service dog does not do! This means you should not leave enticing food on kitchen tables or counters when you are not around. Even if you think the counter or table is high enough to where your dog can't reach. However, after working diligently on the "leave it" command, you should be able to leave food on the counters and tables while you are in the kitchen.

Just like you did with food on the ground, you will want to train your dog to obey your "leave it" command when you place food on a kitchen table or counter. In this exercise, have a book or something similar ready to bang on the counter, or you can use a "shake can." You want to make a loud noise when your dog approaches the food on the counter to get your dog to back away.

Make sure to praise enthusiastically when he backs away. You should also apply this training to lower tables as well. Eventually, you want to see how obedient your dog is when he is off-leash. You will want to practice with food on the table while your dog is off-leash, but have a friend ready to pick up and move the food if your dog doesn't obey your "leave it" command while he is off-leash.

Chapter 15: next steps

"you only grow by coming to the end of something and by beginning something else."

-John Irving

If you've made it this far, and you've applied the steps and methods in this book, then you have a reliable, well-trained companion that is easy to live with. You have done something very few people manage to do. I know it was frustrating at times, but the results should be well worth it with enough patience.

However, the journey doesn't necessarily end here. If you plan to train a service dog, know finishing this book is just the first step. A lot more your dog can learn as a service dog and a lot more your dog will need to learn to be not just a service dog but a super service dog.

However, we have reached the end of what this book covers. If you want to continue the journey of training a super service dog, you will need volume 2 of this series, where we cover many other commands your dog can learn, how to prepare for the public access test, and much more.

In volume 2, we will also discuss adding distractions to the basic obedience exercise because a service dog has to be able to perform all these exercises in public where there will likely be a lot of distractions especially given how good a dog's hearing is. You will want to slowly expose your dog to public spaces in as controlled of circumstances as you can. It's important not to overwhelm your dog when you first take your dog out to public places.

So, you want to think before you go out. Is there a big event going on at the park today? Will the mall be extra crowded this weekend? These are the types of questions you want to ask yourself before you start taking your dog out in public for the first few times. As usual, it is important to start slowly. When you take your dog to a new environment, it may seem like your dog has never heard your command words before. This is because your dog is not used to hearing your commands in a new environment.

So, you will want to start at the beginning with each exercise in each new location. Your dog will likely catch up very quickly because you've helped your dog learn how to learn. Always remember patience is key. Also, make sure to use food rewards and lots of praise.

It's good to start practicing all the obedience commands in your backyard, then move into your front yard, where you might find more distractions. Be patient and use praise to get your dog's attention and to keep it on you. Make sure to follow through on each command. This means if you give your dog your "sit" command, make sure he sits and don't proceed until he does. Remember to use food treats just as you did when you first practiced these exercises.

When your dog promptly follows your commands in the front yard, you can move to a quiet park or schoolyard. Practice for several sessions, going through all of your obedience commands. Even if your dog doesn't perform the exercise as accurately as he does at home, still make sure to give appropriate praise and treats when he does it correctly. With patience and consistent practice, your dog will be just as precise with the commands in public as he is at home. Keep realistic expectations and don't expect a perfect execution of the commands the first time practicing in public.

After several sessions in the quiet park, you can next move to an area like a mall or shopping center. One thing you need to be aware of when practicing more urban environments like this is the temperature of the pavement. Never work on the blacktop when it's hot outside. Not only are dogs very sensitive to heat, but your dog doesn't have shoes on his paws as you do on your feet so that a hot blacktop can be highly uncomfortable for your dog.

When your dog is confidently carrying out the basic obedience commands, stand with your dog near the entrance to a busy store. Give your dog your "sit" or "down" command, so he is in the sit or down position as people pass by. If someone wants to pet your dog, remember you have the right to say no, and you should say no until you have done this exercise several times. Makes sure to prevent strangers from crowding around your dog.

You want this exercise to be a positive experience for your dog, and you want to maintain control, so if people approach you and your dog, let them know that your dog is training to become a service dog, and he can't be petted right now. Once you know you have good control, you can allow one person to approach your dog.

Your dog shouldn't back away to greet a person, nor should your dog jump up to greet a person. Your dog should remain in the "sit" or "down" position. It may take weeks or even months to accomplish this.

If your dog is shy, you must make sure not to overwhelm him. You have to build up your dog's confidence slowly to help him overcome his shyness. This could take up to months of diligent work. On the other hand, if you have an aggressive dog, do not even consider taking him out in public. Regardless of how much work you put in, you should never trust a dog that consistently shows aggression.

If a service dog bites someone or acts aggressively towards people or other dogs, it will reflect badly on service dogs in general.

Believe it or not, many people don't want dogs around, and they will look for any excuse to get them banned. Taking a service dog out in public is a privilege that carries a great responsibility. You must take this responsibility seriously because many people rely on their service dogs for essential assistance. Anything that reflects poorly on service dogs could make a life for many people more complicated than it already is.

With that being said, you've reached the end of super service dogs: how to train the most supportive service dog and companion volume 1. If you wish to take your dog to the next level and have him or she become a fully-fledged super service dog, then you will want to get volume 2 of this series, where we go more in-depth with the different commands you can teach your dog.

Along with volume 2 of this series, I would highly recommend buying a few journals or logbooks to keep up with your dogs' progress. I have only seen one other logbook made with service dogs besides the ones I have for sale.

Like this series, the logbooks come in 2 parts. One logbook is for the basic commands that we've covered in this book, and the second is for the more advanced commands covered in volume 2. With that being said, this concludes the first steps in your journey of service dog training. I hope you got as much out of reading this book as I did writing it. Until next time I wish the best for you and your super service dog!